THE GOD OF THE KING JAMES BIBLE

JAMES COFFEY

WESTBOW
PRESS®
A DIVISION OF THOMAS NELSON
& ZONDERVAN

This book is a work of non-fiction. Unless otherwise noted, the author and the publisher make no explicit guarantees as to the accuracy of the information contained in this book and in some cases, names of people and places have been altered to protect their privacy.

Scripture taken from the King James Version of the Bible.

WestBow Press books may be ordered through booksellers or by contacting:

WestBow Press
A Division of Thomas Nelson & Zondervan
1663 Liberty Drive
Bloomington, IN 47403
www.westbowpress.com
1 (866) 928-1240

Because of the dynamic nature of the Internet, any web addresses or links contained in this book may have changed since publication and may no longer be valid. The views expressed in this work are solely those of the author and do not necessarily reflect the views of the publisher, and the publisher hereby disclaims any responsibility for them.

Any people depicted in stock imagery provided by Getty Images are models, and such images are being used for illustrative purposes only.
Certain stock imagery © Getty Images.

ISBN: 978-1-9736-4667-9 (sc)
ISBN: 978-1-9736-4668-6 (e)

Print information available on the last page.

WestBow Press rev. date: 7/31/2019

PREFACE

The humble goal of this work is to demonstrate what the Bible teaches about God through the words of the King James Bible. The title of this book does not suggest that the God portrayed in the King James Version differs from the God portrayed in other English versions of the Bible. It simply uses the beautiful, poetic, and hopefully still-familiar words of the King James Bible to reveal who the one true God is.

THE KING JAMES BIBLE—
HOW WE GOT IT AND
WHY IT'S SPECIAL

The King James Bible was the product of the Renaissance and the Reformation. More specifically, it was produced during the height of the English Renaissance and the English Reformation. One can say the King James translation was the culmination of a tremendous spiritual movement that liberated millions from superstition and slavery.

There is certainly no biblical prohibition against translating the Scriptures into another language, yet the Catholic Church and many governments opposed translations of the Bible into the mother tongues of the common people. Laws and intimidation were used to stop these translations, but even intolerant laws and cruel violence could not stop this divine movement of making the Word of God available to large populations.

The first step toward the production of the King James Bible was taken many centuries before its translation. The Septuagint was the rendering of the Hebrew Scriptures into Koine (common) Greek. The Septuagint translation began approximately 250 BC and was completed by about 150 BC. It had a significant influence on the Jewish community to which Jesus and the apostles ministered. The inspired writers of the New Testament (which is also written in Koine Greek) used the Septuagint extensively. The Septuagint set the precedent for rendering the Word of God into another language.

The next significant translation was the Latin Vulgate. Saint Jerome translated the Bible into Latin. He rendered the Old Testament from Hebrew into Latin and the New Testament from Greek into Latin. Jerome's Vulgate became the Bible of the Roman Catholic Church, and its reign lasted for over a thousand years.

The Vulgate was the foundation of Medieval intellectual life. Many great universities were started at this time: Oxford, Cambridge, Paris, Bologna, and Padua. However, as time went by, Latin became primarily the language of scholars. Most Europeans did not speak or read Latin, especially the Latin of the fourth-century Vulgate. Thus, the Bible, in effect, was not available to the common people.

John Wycliffe, an English theologian, saw the need for the Bible to be translated into the language of his people. Wycliffe saw two reasons for this translation: (1) The people needed salvat ion and enlightenment; and (2) the Roman Catholic Church was corrupt, and the best way to reveal that corruption was comparing church doctrine and practices to the teachings of Scripture. However, Wycliffe's translation was limited by two factors. First, he translated from the Latin Vulgate, not from the original Hebrew and Greek. Second, since the printing press had not yet been invented, all of Wycliffe's Bibles were hand-copied.

In 1453 Ottoman Turks captured Constantinople, marking the end of the Byzantine Empire. As a result of this victory for Islam, thousands of Christians fled to the West. They brought with them thousands of Greek New Testament manuscripts, including some of the oldest and best copies. These manuscripts created a renaissance in the study of Greek and the New Testament itself.

In 1454 Johannes Guttenberg invented the printing press, and the age of books began. The first book Guttenberg printed was the Latin Vulgate.

Gerson ben Moses Soncino, a Jewish printer, published the full Hebrew Bible in 1494. Martin Luther used a Soncino Hebrew Bible to translate the Old Testament from Hebrew into German.

Desiderius Erasmus published the Greek New Testament in 1516. Erasmus's Greek New Testament was the foundation for the Textus Receptus, the Greek text used by the men who translated the King James Bible.

On October 31, 1517, Martin Luther posted his Ninety-five Theses on the door of the All-Saints Church in Wittenberg. Luther did not himself have the Ninety-five Theses published; however, several other men had the Theses published and widely distributed throughout Germany. Luther's grievances against the Catholic Church spread quickly and widely throughout Europe, and the Reformation was born. Luther's translation of the entire Bible into German made the Scriptures accessible to the common people in their own language.

The Complutensian Polyglot Bible, published in 1520, was a remarkable achievement, for it contained the Hebrew Bible, the Greek Septuagint, and the Latin Vulgate. The three-language texts appeared on the same page, where they could be compared. This greatly aided the teaching of biblical Hebrew and Greek.

When England's Catholic king Henry VIII wanted to divorce Catherine of Aragon, his first wife, the pope would not permit him to do so. So, Henry initiated the break of the English church from the Roman Catholic Church. The king replaced the pope as head of the Church in England. England almost overnight went from a Catholic majority country to a Protestant majority nation.

William Tyndale was a brilliant man and a great writer. During the reign of Henry VIII, Tyndale sought permission from the bishop of London to translate the Bible into English. (This was before Henry VIII had split from Rome.) The Catholic bishop of London never permitted Tyndale to start his translation, so Tyndale finally left England and went to Europe. There he produced a wonderful English translation of the Greek New Testament. Tyndale's New Testament had to be smuggled into England; however, it was a big success. Henry VIII, still a loyal Catholic at the time, was not pleased.

The king sent royal agents to Europe with orders to find Tyndale and bring him back to England. Tyndale was betrayed by a friend, and Henry's agents arrested him. Instead of bringing him back to England, however, the agents let local officials and the Catholic Church take control of Tyndale. They executed him by strangulation and then had his body burned at the stake. When Henry learned of this, he was furious. He had wanted Tyndale brought back to him, and by this time, Henry was in full rebellion against the Catholic Church.

Miles Coverdale also produced an English translation of the Bible. His New Testament was almost the same as Tyndale's. His Old Testament was not a translation from the Hebrew. Rather, Coverdale took Martin Luther's Old Testament written in German and translated it into English.

When Henry VIII died, his young son, Edward, became king. Although Edward did not live long, during his reign, the Protestant Reformation begun by Henry took deeper root.

When Edward died, Mary ascended to the throne. She was the daughter of Henry and his first wife, Catherine of Aragon. Mary was not pleased with the way her mother had been treated. She was very Roman Catholic, and she was married to Philip of Spain, a defender of the Catholic faith.

Mary tried to reverse the Protestant Reformation in England. She killed so many Protestants that she became known as "Bloody Mary." Her persecution of Protestants cemented the Protestant Reformation in England. For many generations to come, the British people associated Catholicism with Mary's harsh reign. Mary died without issue, and Elizabeth took her place on the throne.

Elizabeth was a brilliant woman—as much so as her father Henry VIII. She was Protestant and very much strengthened the Church of England, but she rejected more thorough reforms in the church sought by the Puritans. Elizabeth was a nationalist. England became a powerful nation under her rule. Protestant scholarship in the universities flourished. The men who would translate the King James Bible were educated during this time. They learned Hebrew and Greek, and they started their careers teaching in the great universities of England. They were all Protestants.

When Elizabeth's navy defeated the Spanish Armada in 1588, Protestantism in England was cemented. There was no going back.

Two English Bible translations were completed during Elizabeth's reign. One was primarily the work of James Parker, the Archbishop of Canterbury. The second was the Geneva Bible, which soon eclipsed Parker's translation.

The Geneva Bible was a significant advance in Bible translation and printing. It was called the Geneva Bible because the translation work was done in Geneva, Switzerland. It was translated from the Hebrew and Greek, and it was written in the language of the English people. It was not a Latinized English as so many Bible translations before, and its appearance was similar in size to the Bibles in print today. Up until the Geneva Bible, Bibles were huge in size.

When it was smuggled into England a year before Mary's death, it caught on like cake in a famine. Henry VIII probably would have suppressed the Geneva Bible. Mary the First certainly would have burned it. Elizabeth, however, admired it. She knew it was a great intellectual work and superior to the Parker Bible.

The Geneva Bible was the Bible of William Shakespeare, the greatest of all English writers/poets. King James VI of Scotland, however, did not like the Geneva Bible because of its marginal notes. These notes were very pro-liberty and anti-tyranny, and James viewed them as a threat to his rule.

Elizabeth died without children, and King James VI was chosen to replace her on the throne of England. Puritans in England had high hopes for James's coming reign. They viewed him as a Protestant of Protestants because he was raised by Presbyterians in Scotland. They did not know that although James was a sincere Protestant, he did not really like Presbyterianism. He believed Presbyterianism would lead to the end of the monarchy—that it was too "grassroots" in its form of government. James wanted a top-down style of government, one where he, as king, was head of church and state.

Even before his coronation, the English Puritans presented to James their grievances and reforms for the Church of England. James was not about to give into them; however, he did agree to a convention at Hope House in the fall of 1604.

At the Hope Convention, James granted only one concession to the Puritans, and that request was for a new translation of the Bible. It would be officially authorized by King James, and it would be the Bible of the Church of England. The best minds in England would translate it—one group would translate the Hebrew Old Testament, another group the Greek New Testament, and a third group the Apocrypha from the Greek Septuagint. They would do the translation work in peace and free of persecution. Unlike William Tyndale, these scholars did not have worry about being strangled to death for simply translating the Scriptures.

The translators' goal was a readable and accurate Bible translation for the English people. They wanted a Bible that was good for oral reading. They worked very hard at this, spending hours and hours reading the Bible to each other to make sure the people could understand it and that the language would be metrical, even poetic. Their rendering of the book of Psalms is one of the great masterpieces of human civilization.

When people say the King James Bible is not in modern English, they are wrong. The King James was translated into early-modern English. It is not the Old English of *Beowulf* or the Middle English of *The*

Canterbury Tales. Shakespeare wrote *Hamlet* in 1609, while the King James Bible was completed in 1611. It is, in essence, the same beautiful language, and the same English worldview. No modern translation can match the King James translation of the book of Psalms. They pale in comparison. The Psalms of the King James is true poetry. The Psalms of contemporary translations are just prose written in pseudo-poetic form. During the age of King James, the psalms were sung in English churches. The poetic language of the King James Bible is superior to any of the modern translations, especially the dynamic-equivalent translations.

Most surveys of English literature include the King James Bible because it is regarded by literature teachers as one of the great works of literature, equal to *The Canterbury Tales, Hamlet, Romeo and Juliet, Paradise Lost,* and many others. Of course, since the King James Bible is the Word of God, we would say it is superior to those other works of literature.

Harold Bloom, one of America's foremost authorities on literature, wrote *The Shadow of a Great Rock,* in which he delineates the linguistic greatness and profound influence of the King James Bible. The King James Bible also made Bloom's "Western canon," his list of the greatest works of literature in the history of Western civilization.

Sections of the King James are also included in many English Literature anthologies because of its profound influence on the history of English language and culture. It influenced the development of the English language in England and America.

The men who translated the King James Bible were geniuses, the best minds in England—even in Europe. They had a truly Christian, genuinely Protestant worldview. They knew the Bible was the inspired Word of God. They were not corrupted by evolution, Marxism, multiculturalism, racism, or sexual perversion. Today even so-called "Christian" people attack the Bible. In the era of the translation of the King James Bible, no one would not dare attack the Bible.

Simply put, the age of the King James Bible was a more godly age than our twenty-first-century world. In seventeenth-century England, no one was writing books advocating that "Jesus had a wife," or that occult practices are acceptable in the church, or that marriage is something other than the union of a man and a woman. The King James Bible was a product of a better world.

THE KING JAMES BIBLE TEACHES THAT THERE IS ONLY ONE GOD

"Unto thee it was shewed, that thou mightest know that the LORD he is God; there is none else beside him" (Deuteronomy 4:35).

"Know therefore this day, and consider it in thine heart, that the LORD he is God in heaven above, and upon the earth beneath: there is none else" (Deuteronomy 4:39).

"Hear, O Israel: The LORD our God is one LORD: And thou shalt love the LORD thy God with all thine heart, and with all thy soul, and with all thy might" (Deuteronomy 6:4-5).

"See now that I, even I, am he, and there is no god with me: I kill, and I make alive; I wound, and I heal: neither is there any that can deliver out of my hand" (Deuteronomy 32:39).

"There is none holy as the LORD: for there is none beside thee: neither is there any rock like our God (1 Samuel 2:2).

"Wherefore thou art great, O LORD God: for there is none like thee, neither is there any God beside thee, according to all that we have heard with our ears" (2 Samuel 7:22).

"That men may know that thou, whose name alone is JEHOVAH, art the most high over all the earth" (Psalm 83:18).

"For thou art great, and doest wondrous things: thou art God alone" (Psalm 86:10).

"Ye are my witnesses, saith the LORD, and my servant whom I have chosen: that ye may know and believe me, and understand the I am he: before me there was no God formed, neither shall there be after me (Isaiah 43:10).

"Thus saith the LORD the King of Israel, and his redeemer the LORD of hosts; I am the first, and I am the last; and beside me there is no God" (Isaiah 44:6).

"Look unto me, and be ye saved, all the ends of the earth: for I am God, and there is none else (Isaiah 45:22).

The New Testament agrees with the Old Testament: there is only one God.

"And Jesus answered him, The first of all commandments is, Hear, O Israel; The Lord our God is one Lord" (Mark 12:29).

"And the scribe said unto him, Well, Master, thou hast said the truth: for there is one God; and there is none other but he" (Mark 12:32).

"How can ye believe, which receive honour one of another, and seek not the honour that cometh from God only" (John 5:44).

"I and my Father are one" (John 10:30).

"And this is life eternal, that they might know thee the only true God, and Jesus Christ, whom thou hast sent" (John 17:3).

"Is he the God of the Jews only? Is he not also of the Gentiles? Yes, of the Gentiles also: Seeing it is one God, which shall justify the circumcision by faith, and uncircumcision through faith" (Romans 3:29-30).

"As concerning therefore the eating of those things that are offered in sacrifice unto idols, we know that an idol is nothing in the world, and that there is none other God but one. . . . But to us there is but one God, the Father, of whom are all things, and we in him; and one Lord Jesus, by whom are all things, and we by him" (1 Corinthians 8:4, 6).

"There is one body, and one Spirit, even as ye are called in one hope of your calling; One Lord, one faith, one baptism; One God and Father of all, who is above all, and through all, and in you all" (Ephesians 4:4-6)

"For there is one God, and one mediator between God and men, the man Christ Jesus" (1 Timothy 2:5).

"Thou believest that there is one God; thou doest well: the devils also believe, and tremble" (James 2:19).

"For there are three that bear record in heaven, the Father, the Word, and the Holy Ghost: and these three are one" (1 John 5:7). [This exact wording of 1 John 5:7 is found only in the King James translation.]

THE KING JAMES BIBLE TEACHES THAT GOD IS THE SAME GOD IN BOTH TESTAMENTS

"And I say unto you, That many shall come from the east and west, and shall sit down with Abraham and Isaac and Jacob, in the kingdom of heaven" (Matthew 8:11).

"Your father Abraham rejoiced to see my day: and he saw it, and was glad" (John 8:56).

"Verily, Verily I say unto you, Before Abraham was, I am" (John 8:58).

"These things said Esaias, when he saw his (Jesus') glory, and spake of him" (John 12:41).

"But this I confess unto thee, that after the way, which they call heresy, so worship I the God of my fathers, believing all things which are written in the law and in the prophets (Acts 24:14).

"To Timothy, my dearly beloved son: Grace, mercy, and peace, from God the Father and Christ Jesus our Lord. I thank God, whom I serve from my forefathers with pure conscience, that without ceasing I have remembrance of thee in my prayers day and night" (2 Timothy 1:2-3).

THE GOD OF THE KING JAMES BIBLE IS ETERNAL, WITH LIFE IN HIMSELF

God always existed and is the ultimate reality. The physical universe is not the paramount reality—God is.

> "In the beginning God created the heaven and the earth" (Genesis 1:1).

> "Before the mountains were brought forth, or ever thou hadst formed the earth and the world, even from everlasting to everlasting, thou art God" (Psalm 90:2).

> "Thy throne is established of old: thou art from everlasting" (Psalm 93:2).

> "And God said unto Moses I AM THAT I AM: and he said, Thus shall thou say unto the children of Israel, I AM hath sent me unto you" Exodus 3:14.

> "Jesus said unto them, Verily, Verily, I say unto you, Before Abraham I am" (John 8:58).

The "I am" statements in the Bible are God's ultimate statement about His eternal self-existence. God always existed, and He was the only thing that did exist until the Creation. The angels did not exist. Man did not exist. The earth did not exist. The universe did not exist. Time did not exist.

God was not alone because God is a tri-unity. He is One God in three Persons: God the Father, God the Son, and God the Holy Spirit. The Father, Son, and Holy Spirit had perfect fellowship for all eternity past. That is why Moses called God "the eternal God" (Deuteronomy 33:27).

Judaism and Islam teach that God is one person. However, if God were one person, He would have dwelt alone for all eternity past—a very lonely person. But God said of Adam, who was made in God's image, that it was "not good that the man should be alone; I will make him an help meet for him" (Genesis 2:18).

Here are some other King James Bible verses concerning God's eternality and self-existence:

> "For thus saith the high and lofty One that inhabiteth eternity, whose name is Holy; I dwell in the high and holy place, with him also that is of a contrite and humble spirit, to revive the spirit of the humble, and to revive the heart of the contrite ones" Isaiah 57:15.

> "Hast thou not known? Hast thou not heard, that the everlasting God, the LORD, the Creator of the ends of the earth, fainteth not, neither is weary? There is no searching of his understanding" (Isaiah 40:28).

> "Ye are my witnesses, saith the LORD, and my servant whom I have chosen: that ye may know and believe me, and understand that I *am* he: before me there was no God formed, neither shall there be after me" (Isaiah 43:10).

Daniel's vision of the Son of Man and the Ancient of days:

> "I beheld till the thrones were cast down, and the Ancient of days did sit, whose garment was white as snow, and the hair of his head like the pure wool: his throne was like the fiery flame, and his wheels as burning fire" (Daniel 7:9).

> "I saw in the night visions, and, behold, one like the Son of man came to the Ancient of days, and they brought him near before him" (Daniel 7:13).

The prophecy of the birth of Christ:

> "But thou, Bethlehem Ephratah, though thou be little among the thousands of Judah, yet out of thee shall he come forth unto me that is to be ruler in Israel; whose goings forth have been from of old, from everlasting" (Micah 5:2).

As the eternal God, Christ always existed with the Father. And all things were created by Christ.

> "In the beginning was the Word, and the Word was with God, and the Word was God . . . All things were made by him; and without him was not any thing made that was made" (John 1:1-3).

> "And the four beasts had each of them six wings about him; and they were full of eyes within: and they rest not day and night, saying, Holy, holy, holy, Lord

God Almighty, which was, and is, and is to come" (Revelation 4:8).

Just as the Father is eternal and has life in Himself (not created), so the Son is eternal and has life in Himself. They both are ever-living and eternal.

> "For as the Father hath life in himself; so hath he given to the Son to have life in himself" (John 5:26).

> "And now, O Father, glorify thou me with thine own self with the glory which I had with thee before the world was" (John 17:5).

The eternal, ever-living God is the One from whom all life and existence come:

> "Neither is worshipped with men's hands, as though he needed any thing, seeing he giveth to all life, and breath, and all things" (Acts 17:25).

Again, all things came from God. All things exist for God. All things exist by His power.

> "For of him, and through him, and to him, are all things: to whom be glory for ever. Amen" (Romans 11:36).

> "And he [Christ] is before all things, and by him all things consist" (Colossians 1:17).

"God . . . Hath in these last days spoken unto us by his Son, whom he hath appointed heir of all things, by whom also he made the worlds; Who being the brightness of his glory, and the express image of his person, and upholding all things by the word of his power, when he had by himself purged our sins, sat down on the right hand of the Majesty on high" (Hebrews 1:1-3).

"For it became him, for whom are all things, and by whom are all things, in bringing many sons unto glory, to make the captain of their salvation perfect through sufferings" (Hebrew 2:10.

"I am Alpha and Omega, the beginning and the ending, saith the Lord, which is, and which was, and which is to come, the Almighty" (Revelation 1:8).

"And, behold, I come quickly; and my reward is with me, to give every man according as his work shall be. I am Alpha and Omega, the beginning and the end, the first and the last" (Revelation 22:12-13).

THE GOD OF THE KING JAMES BIBLE IS THE CREATOR

One of the best aspects of the King James Bible is that all the men who translated it were young-earth creationists. None of them believed in evolution. They did their translation work 248 years before Darwin. The uniquely Christian/creationist worldview of the King James Bible is one of its greatest strengths.

The God of the King James Bible is the Creator of the universe, the earth, man, and all life on earth—everything. The truth that God is the Creator is interwoven throughout the Bible.

> "In the beginning God created the heaven and the earth" (Genesis 1:1).

God did not use great periods of time. He did it in six literal days, and He rested on the seventh day.

> "But the seventh day is the Sabbath of the LORD thy God: in it thou shalt not do any work, thou, nor thy son, nor thy daughter, thy manservant, not thy maidservant, nor thy cattle, nor thy stranger that is within thy gates: For in six days the Lord made heaven and earth, the sea, and all that in them is, and rested on the seventh day: wherefore the LORD blessed the sabbath day, and hallowed it" (Exodus 20:10-11).

"By the word of the LORD were the heavens made; and the host of them by the breath of his month" (Psalm 33:6).

"Thou, even thou, are LORD alone; thou hast made heaven, the heaven of heavens, with all their host, the earth, and all things that are therein, the seas, and all that is therein, and thou preservest them all; and the host of heaven worshippeth thee" Nehemiah 9:6.

"He stretcheth out the north over the empty place, and hangeth the earth upon nothing" (Job 26:7).

"I have made the earth, and created man upon it: I, even my hands, have stretched out the heavens, and their host have I commanded" (Isaiah 45:12)

"All things were made by him (Christ); and without him was not any thing made that was made" (John 1:3).

"And saying, Sirs, why do ye these things? We also are men of like passions with you, and preach unto you that ye should turn from these vanities unto the living God, which made heaven, and earth, and the sea, and all things that are therein" (Acts 14:15).

"But to us there is but one God, the Father, of whom are all things, and we in him; and one Lord Jesus Christ, by whom are all things, and we by him" (1 Corinthians 8:6).

"For by him (Christ) were all things created, that are in heaven, and that are in earth, visible and invisible, whether they be thrones, or dominions, or principalities, or powers; all things were created by him, and for him: and he is before all things, and by him all things consist" (Colossians 1:16-17).

"Through faith we understand that the worlds were framed by the word of God, so that things which are seen were not made of things which do appear" (Hebrews 11:3).

"Thou art worthy, O Lord, to receive glory and honour and power: for thou hast created all things, and for thy pleasure they are and were created" (Revelation 4:11).

THE GOD OF THE KING JAMES BIBLE IS SOVEREIGN

"The LORD hath prepared his throne in the heavens; and his kingdom ruleth over all" (Psalm 103:19).

"The LORD reigneth; let the earth rejoice; let the multitude of isles be glad thereof" (Psalm 97:1).

"The LORD reigneth; let the people tremble: he sitteth between the cherubims; let the earth be moved" (Psalm 99:1).

"But our God is in the heavens: he hath done whatsoever he hath pleased" (Psalm 115:3).

"Whatsoever the LORD pleased, that he did in heaven, and in earth, in the seas, and all deep places" (Psalm 135:6).

"The LORD said to my Lord, Sit thou at my right hand, until I make thine enemies thy footstool" (Psalm 110:1).

"The preparations of the heart in man, and the answer of the tongue, is from the LORD" (Proverbs 16:1).

"The LORD hath made all things for himself: yea, even the wicked for the day of evil" (Proverbs 16:4).

The sovereign God controls kings:

"The king's heart is in the hand of the LORD, as the rivers of water: he turneth it whithersoever he will" (Proverbs 21:1).

God hardened Pharaoh's heart:

"And I will harden Pharaoh's heart, and multiply my signs and my wonders in the land of Egypt, but Pharaoh shall not hearken unto you, that I may lay my hand upon Egypt, and bring forth mine armies, and my people, the children of Israel, out of the land of Egypt by great judgements" (Exodus 7:3-5).

The Apostle Paul amplified this idea in Romans 9:17:

"For the scripture saith unto Pharaoh, Even for this same purpose have I raised thee up, that I might shew my power in thee, and that my name might be declared throughout all the earth."

The sovereign God raised up King Cyrus to destroy the Babylonian Empire and rule the ancient world:

"Thus saith the LORD to his anointed, to Cyrus, whose right hand I have holden, to subdue nations before him; and I will loose the loins of kings" (Isaiah 45:1).

The sovereign Lord ended the military expansion of Sennacherib, King of Assyria:

"Be not afraid of the words that thou hast heard, wherewith the servants of the king of Assyria have blasphemed me. Behold I will send a blast upon him, and he shall hear a rumour, and return to his own land; and I will cause him to fall by the sword in his own land" (Isaiah 37:6-7).

God revealed to Daniel that he "changeth the times and the seasons: he removeth kings, and setteth up kings" (Daniel 2:21).

God revealed to Nebuchadnezzar:

"This matter is by the decree of the watchers, and the demand by the word of the holy ones: to the intent that the living may know that the Most High ruleth in the kingdom of men, and giveth it to whomsoever he will, and setteth up over it the basest of men" (Daniel 4:17).

In speaking of Jesus in his great Pentecost sermon, Peter said:

"Him, being delivered by the determined counsel and foreknowledge of God, ye have taken, and by wicked hands have crucified and slain: whom God hath raised up" (Acts 2:23-24).

Paul spoke of God controlling nations and their habitat, saying:

"And (God) hath made of one blood all nations of men for to dwell on all the face of the earth, and hath determined the times before appointed, and bounds of their habitation" (Acts 17:26).

"Let every soul be subject unto the higher powers. For there is no power but of God: the powers that be are ordained of God. Whosoever therefore resisteth the power, resisteth the ordinance of God: and they that resist shall receive to themselves damnation" (Romans 13:1-2).

"Honour all men. Love the brotherhood. Fear God. Honour the king." (1 Peter 2:17).

In Romans 9:19-20 the Apostle Paul likens men's questioning the sovereignty of God to clay pots questioning the actions of their potter-creator:

"Nay but, O man, who art thou that repliest against God? Shall the thing formed say to him that formed it, Why hast thou made me thus? Hath not the potter power over the clay, of the same lump to make one vessel unto honour, and another unto dishonor?"

Long before Paul lived, Job came to the same conclusion:

"I know that thou (God) canst do everything, and that no thought can be withholden from thee . . . therefore have I uttered that I understood not; things too wonderful for me, which I knew not" (Job 42:2-3).

Two great statements about God's sovereignty in salvation are found in Ephesians:

"According as he hath chosen us in him before the foundation of the world, that we should be holy and without blame before him in love: having predestinated us unto the adoption of children by Jesus Christ to himself, according to the good pleasure of his will" (Ephesians 1:4-5).

"In whom (Christ) also we have obtained an inheritance, being predestined according to the purpose of him who worketh all things after the counsel of own will" (Ephesians 1:11).

God's sovereignty should comfort us:

"And Joseph said unto them, Fear not: for am I in the place of God? But as for you, ye thought evil against me; but God meant it unto good, to bring to pass, as it is this day, to save much people alive" (Genesis 50:18-19).

"And we know that all things work together for good to them that love God, to them who are the called according to his purpose" (Romans 8:28).

THE GOD OF THE KING JAMES BIBLE IS HOLY

"So he (God) drove out the man; and he placed at the east of the garden of Eden Cherubims, and a flaming sword which turned everyway, to keep the way of the tree of life" (Genesis 3:24).

"And he (God) said, Draw not nigh hither: put off thy shoes from off thy feet, for the place whereon thou standest is holy ground" (Exodus 3:5).

"Who is like unto thee, O LORD, among the gods? Who is like thee, glorious in holiness, fearful in praises, doing wonders?" (Exodus 15:11).

"And the men of Bethshemesh said, Who is able to stand before this holy LORD God?" (1 Samuel 6:20).

"The LORD is great in Zion; and he is high above all the people. Exalt the LORD our God, and worship at his holy hill; for the LORD our God is holy" (Psalm 99:2, 9).

"The fear of the LORD is the beginning of wisdom: and the knowledge of the holy is understanding" (Proverbs 9:10).

"And one cried unto another and said, Holy, holy, holy, is the LORD of hosts: the whole earth is full of his glory" (Isaiah 6:3).

"So will I make my holy name known in the midst of my people Israel; and I will not let them pollute my holy name any more: and the heathen shall know that I am the LORD, the Holy One in Israel" (Ezekiel 39:7).

Christ's coming into the world was an act of holiness:

"And the angel answered and said unto her, The Holy Ghost shall come upon thee, and the power of the Highest shall overshadow thee: therefore also that holy thing which shall be born of thee shall be called the Son of God" (Luke 1:35).

"And the Holy Ghost descended in a bodily shape like a dove upon him, and a voice came from heaven, which said, Thou art my beloved Son; in thee I am well pleased" (Luke 3:22).

"And now I am no more in the world, but these, Holy Father, keep through thine own name (YHWH) those whom thou hast given me, that they may be one, as we are" (John 17:11).

"O righteous Father, the world hath not known thee: but I have known thee, and these have known that thou hast sent me" (John 17:25).

"Follow peace with all men, and holiness, without which no man shall see the Lord" (Hebrews 12:14).

"But as he which hath called you is holy, so be ye holy in all manner of conversation; because it is written, Be YE HOLY; FOR I AM HOLY" (1 Peter 1:15-16).

"For the prophecy came not in old time by the will of man: but holy men of God spake as they were moved by the Holy Ghost" (2 Peter 1:21).

"And the four beasts had each of them six wings about him; and they were full of eyes within: and they rest not day and night, saying, Holy, holy, holy, Lord God Almighty, which was, and is, and is to come" (Revelation 4:8).

THE GOD OF THE KING JAMES BIBLE IS SPIRIT

"In the beginning God created the heaven and the earth. . . . And the Spirit of God moved upon the face of the water" (Genesis 1:1-2).

"And the LORD said, My spirit shall not always strive with man, for he also is flesh: yet his days shall be an hundred and twenty years" (Genesis 6:3).

"But the Spirit of the LORD departed from Saul, and an evil spirit from the LORD troubled him" (1 Samuel 16:14).

"Cast me not away from thy presence; and take not thy holy spirit from me" (Psalm 51:11)

"The Spirit of the Lord GOD is upon me; because the LORD hath anointed me to preach good tidings unto the meek; he hath sent me to bind up the brokenhearted, to proclaim liberty to the captives, and the opening of the prison to them that are bound" (Isaiah 61:1; Luke 4:18).

"And Jesus returned in the power of the Spirit into Galilee: and there went out a fame of him through all the region round about" (Luke 4:14)

"And Jesus, when he was baptized, went up straightway out of the water: and, lo, the heavens were opened unto him, and he saw the Spirit of God descending like a dove, and lighting upon him: And lo a voice from heaven, saying, This is my beloved Son, in whom I am well pleased" (Matthew 3:16-17).

"God is a Spirit: and they that worship him must worship him in spirit and in truth" (John 4:24).

"And I will pray the Father, and he shall give you another Comforter, that he may abide with you forever; even the Spirit of truth; whom the world cannot receive, because it seeth him not, neither knoweth him: but ye know him; for he dwelleth with you, and shall be in you" (John 14:16-17).

"And they were all filled with the Holy Ghost, and began to speak with other tongues, as the Spirit gave them utterance" (Acts 2:4).

"As they ministered to the Lord, and fasted, the Holy Ghost said, Separate me Barnabas and Saul for the work whereunto I have called them" (Acts 13:2).

"But God hath revealed them unto us by his Spirit: for the Spirit searcheth all things, yea, the deep things of God. For what man knoweth the things of a man, save the spirit of man which is in him? Even so the things of God knoweth no man, but the Spirit of God" (1 Corinthians 2:10-11).

"The Grace of the Lord Jesus Christ, and the love of God, and the communion of the Holy Ghost, be with you all. Amen" (2 Corinthians 13:14).

"Furthermore, we have had fathers of our flesh which corrected us, and we gave them reverence: shall we not much rather be in subjection unto the Father of spirits, and live?" (Hebrews 12:9).

"For we are the circumcision, which worship God in the spirit, and rejoice in Christ Jesus, and have no confidence in the flesh" (Philippians 3:3).

"And the Spirit and the bride say, Come" (Revelation 22:17).

THE GOD OF THE KING JAMES BIBLE IS OMNIPRESENT

"Know therefore this day, and consider it in thine heart, that the LORD he is God in heaven above, and upon the earth beneath: there is none else" (Deuteronomy 4:39).

"But will God indeed dwell on the earth? behold, the heaven and heaven of heavens cannot contain thee; how much less this house that I have builded?" (1 Kings 8:27).

God Himself amplifies this idea:

"Thus saith the LORD, The heaven is my throne, and the earth is my footstool: where is the house that ye build unto me? and where is the place for my rest?" (Isaiah 66:1).

"Hell is naked before him, and destruction hath no covering" (Job 26:6).

"The eyes of the LORD are in every place, beholding the evil and the good" (Proverbs 15:3).

Nathanael experienced that "the eyes of the LORD are in every place" with the Lord Jesus Christ in John 1:48-49:

"Nathanael saith unto him (Jesus), Whence knowest thou me? Jesus answered and said unto him, Before that Philip called thee, when thou wast under the fig tree, I saw thee. Nathanael answered and saith unto him, Rabbi, thou art the Son of God; thou art the King of Israel."

"Whither shall I go from thy spirit? or whither shall I flee from thy presence? If I ascend up into heaven, thou art there: if I make my bed in hell, behold, thou art there. If I take the wings of the morning, and dwell in the uttermost parts of the sea; even there shall thy hand lead me, and thy right hand shall hold me" (Psalm 139:7-10).

"Am I a God at hand, saith the LORD, and not a God afar off? Can any hide himself in secret places that I shall not see him? saith the LORD. Do not I fill heaven and earth? saith the LORD" (Jeremiah 23:23-24).

God's omnipresence encourages men and women to pray:

"But thou, when thou prayest, enter into thy closet, and when thou hast shut thy door, pray to thy Father which is in secret; and thy Father which seeth in secret shall reward thee" (Matthew 6:6).

This is similar to Hagar's experience in Genesis 16:13:

> "And she called the name of the LORD that spake unto her, Thou God seest me: for she said, Have I also here looked after him that seeth me?"

The Apostle Paul told the Athenians about the omnipresence of God:

> "God that made the world and all things therein, seeing that he is Lord of heaven and earth, dwelleth not in temples made with hands. . . . That they (men) should seek the Lord, if haply they might feel after him, and find him, though he be not far from every one of us: for in him we live, and move, and have our being" (Acts 17:24-28).

The Lord Jesus Christ Himself declared that He is omnipresent:

> "For where two or three are gathered together in my name, there am I in the midst of them" (Matthew 18:20).

> "Teaching them to observe all things whatsoever I have commanded you: and, lo, I am with you always, even unto the end of the world. Amen" (Matthew 28:20).

Jesus used His omnipresence to see Nathanael sitting under the fig tree:

> "Jesus answered and said unto him, Before Philip called thee, when thou wast under the fig tree, I saw thee" (John 1:48).

The entire universe is held together by Christ:

> "And he is before all things, and by him all things consist" (Colossians 1:17).

Christ is in all believers:

> "To whom God would make known what is the riches of the glory of this mystery among the Gentiles; which is Christ in you, the hope of glory" (Colossians 1:27).

Not only is Christ in all believers, but all believers are in Christ:

> "To the saints and faithful brethren in Christ" (Colossians1:2).

How can this be if Christ is not omnipresent? Because Christ is omnipresent, all believers have fellowship with Him:

> "That which we have seen and heard declare we unto you, that ye also may have fellowship with us; and truly our fellowship is with the Father, and with his Son Jesus Christ" (1 John 1:3).

Christ walks "in the midst" of all light-bearing churches. He is the One "who walketh in the midst of the seven golden candlesticks" (Revelation 2:1). [In Revelation 1:20 John identifies the seven golden candlesticks as churches.]

The omnipresent Christ knocks on the door of human hearts throughout the globe:

"Behold I stand at the door: if any man hear my voice, and open the door, I will come in to him, and will sup with him, and he with me" (Revelation 3:20).

Paul tells all believers to rejoice because the Lord Jesus "is at hand" (Philippians 4:5).

Christ transcends the physical dimensions:

"That Christ may dwell in your hearts by faith; that ye, being rooted and grounded in love, may be able to comprehend with all saints what is the breadth, and length, and depth, and height; and to know the love of Christ, which passeth knowledge, that ye might be filled with all the fullness of God" (Ephesians 3:17-18).

Jesus Christ promised to be with His children always:

"And lo, I am with you always, even unto the end of the world" (Matthew 28:20).

"I will never leave thee, nor forsake thee" (Hebrews 13:5).

THE GOD OF THE KING JAMES BIBLE IS OMNISCIENT

"Dost thou know the balancing of the clouds, the wondrous works of him (God) which is perfect in knowledge?" (Job 37:16).

"Talk no more so exceeding proudly; let not arrogancy come out of your mouth; for the LORD is a God of knowledge, and by him actions are weighed" (1Samuel 2:3).

"Hast thou not known? Hast thou not heard, that the everlasting God, the LORD, the Creator of the ends of the earth, fainteth not, neither is weary? There is no searching of his understanding" (Isaiah 40:28).

"Great is our Lord, and of great power: his understanding is infinite" (Psalm 147:5).

"For if our heart condemn us, God is greater than our hearts, and knoweth all things" (1 John 3:20).

"His disciples said unto him . . . now are we sure that thou knowest all things" (John 16:29-30).

"In whom [Christ] are hid all the treasures of wisdom and knowledge" (Colossians 2:3).

"But Jesus did not commit himself unto them, because he knew all men. And needed not that any should testify of man: for he knew what was in man" (John 2:24-25).

"Lord, thou knowest all things; thou knowest that I love thee" (John 21:17).

"Come, see a man, which told me all things that I ever did; is not this the Christ?" (John 4:29).

"O the depth of the riches both of the wisdom and knowledge of God! How unsearchable are his judgements, and his ways past finding out! For who hath know the mind of the Lord? Or who hath been his counsellor?" (Romans 11:33-34).

"For my thoughts are not your thoughts, neither are your ways my ways, saith the LORD. For as the heavens are higher than the earth, so are my ways higher than your ways, and my thoughts than your thoughts" (Isaiah 55:8-9).

"And they prayed, and said, Thou, Lord, which knowest the hearts of all men" (Acts 1:24)

"But it is written, EYE HATH NOT SEEN, NOR EAR HEARD, NEITHER HAVE ENTERED INTO THE HEART OF MAN, THE THINGS WHICH GOD HATH PREPARED FOR THEM THAT LOVE HIM. But God hath revealed them unto us by his Spirit: for the Spirit searcheth all things, yea, the deep things of God. For what man knoweth the things of a man, save the spirit of man which is in him? Even so the things of God knoweth no man, but the Spirit of God" (1 Corinthians 2:9-11).

"For WHO HATH KNOWN THE MIND OF THE LORD, THAT HE MAY INSTRUCT HIM? But we have the mind of Christ" (1 Corinthians 2:16).

There are trillions and trillions of stars, yet the omniscient God knows their exact number and has named them all:

"He telleth the number of the starts; he calleth them all by their names. Great is our Lord, and of great power: his understanding is infinite" (Psalm 147:4-5).

"Lift up your eyes on high, and behold who hath created these things, that bringeth out their host by number: he calleth them all by names by the greatness of his might, for he is strong in power; not one faileth" (Isaiah 40:26).

God numbers the hairs on our heads:

"But even the very hairs of your head are all numbered." (Luke 12:7).

The Lord knows all the small things:

"Are not five sparrows sold for two farthings, and not of one them is forgotten before God?" (Luke 12:6)

Nothing is hidden from the light of God's knowledge:

"He revealeth the deep and secret things; he knoweth what is in the darkness, and the light dwelleth with him" (Daniel 2:22).

Knowledge comes from the mind of God:

> "The fear of the LORD is the beginning of knowledge: but fools despise wisdom and instruction" (Proverbs 1:7).

> "The fear of the LORD is the beginning of wisdom, and the knowledge of the holy is understanding" (Proverbs 9:10).

> Jesus is the power and wisdom of God: "But unto them which are called both Jews and Greeks, Christ the power and wisdom of God" (1 Corinthians 2:24).

In Christ "are hid all the treasures of wisdom and knowledge" (Colossians 2:3).

THE GOD OF THE KING JAMES BIBLE IS A PERSON

It is absurd to debate whether or not God, the Creator of both angels and men, is a Person. He certainly is. However, in the twenty-first century, many people do not believe God is a Person. They have watched too many *Star Wars* movies, where the Force is a pantheistic force permeating the universe. Or, they have been influenced by Eastern philosophy, Western atheism (evolution and the big bang), or just sheer twenty-first century ignorance.

Renaissance England did not have such problems, which is one reason the King James translation is a uniquely good translation. Renaissance England was truly a Christian nation, where a large majority of the population had a Christian worldview.

If angels and men are beings of persons, then their Maker certainly is a Person.

God has rational thought and expresses His thoughts through language:

> "And God said, Let there be light: and there was light" (Genesis 1:3).

> "For he (God) spake, and it was done; he commanded, and it stood fast" (Psalm 33:9).

"As they ministered to the Lord, and fasted, the Holy Ghost said, Separate me Barnabas and Saul for the work, whereunto I have called them" (Acts 13:2).

God reasons with men:

"Come now, and let us reason together, saith the LORD: though your sins be as scarlet, they shall be white as snow" (Isaiah 1:18).

"And he (Jesus) said unto them, What man shall there be among you, that shall have one sheep, and if it fall into a pit on the sabbath day, will not lay hold on it, and lift it out? How much then is a man better than a sheep? Wherefore it is lawful to do well on the sabbath days" (Matthew 12:11-12).

"I beseech you therefore, brethren, by the mercies of God, that ye present your bodies a living sacrifice, holy acceptable unto God, which is your reasonable service" (Romans 12:1).

"Lo, this only have I found, that God hath made man upright; but they have sought out many inventions" (Ecclesiastes 7:29).

As a Person, God chooses:

"The LORD did not set his love upon you, nor choose you, because ye were more in number than any people; for ye were the fewest of all people" (Deuteronomy 7:7).

"But God hath chosen the foolish things of the world to confound the wise; and God hath chosen the weak things of the world to confound the things which are mighty" (1 Corinthians 1:27).

"According as he hath chosen us in him before the foundation of the world, that we should be holy and without blame before him in love" (Ephesians 1:4).

As a Person, God loves:

"For God so loved the world, that he gave his only begotten Son, that whosoever believeth in him should not perish, but have everlasting life" (John 3:16).

"But God commendeth his love toward us, in that, while we were yet sinners, Christ died for us" (Romans 5:8).

"For I the LORD thy God will hold thy right hand, saying unto thee, Fear not; I will help thee (Isaiah 41:13).

"He that loveth not knowest not God; for God is love" (1 John 4:8).

As a Person, God teaches:

"Which things also we speak, not in words which man's wisdom teacheth, but which the Holy Ghost teacheth: comparing spiritual things with spiritual" 1 Corinthians 2:13).

"But the Comforter, which is the Holy Ghost, whom the Father will send in my name, he shall teach you all things, and bring all things to your remembrance, whatsoever I have said unto you" (John 14:26).

"But the anointing which ye have received of him (God) abideth in you, and ye need not that any man teach you: but as the same anointing teacheth you of all things, and is truth, and is no lie, and even as it hath taught you, ye shall abide in him" (1 John 2:27).

As a Person, God gets angry:

"And the anger of the LORD was kindled against Moses, and he said, Is not Aaron the Levite thy brother? I know that he can speak well. And also, behold, he cometh forth to meet thee: and when he seeth thee, he will be glad in his heart" (Exodus 4:14).

"For the wrath of God is revealed from heaven against all ungodliness and unrighteousness of men, who hold the truth in unrighteousness" (Romans 1:18).

As a Person, God can be grieved:

"But they rebelled, and vexed his holy Spirit" (Isaiah 63:10).

"He is despised and rejected of men; a man of sorrows, and acquainted with grief" (Isaiah 53:3).

"And grieve not the holy Spirit of God, whereby ye are sealed unto the day of redemption" (Ephesians 4:30).

As a holy Person, God judges:

"Shall the judge of all the earth do right?" (Genesis 19:25).

"For the Father judgeth no man, but hath committed all judgement unto the Son" (John 5:22).

"And as it is appointed unto men once to die, but after this the judgement" (Hebrews 9:27).

Tragically, today many men and women believe in evolution. They believe man is merely a highly evolved animal. The King James Bible teaches that a personal God created men and women in His image. This creation uniquely sets humans apart from the animals and gives them a dignity no other worldview can provide:

"And God said, Let us make man in our image, after our likeness . . . So God created man in his own image, in the image of God created he him; male and female created he them" (Genesis 1:26-27).

THE GOD OF THE KING JAMES BIBLE IS OMNIPOTENT

"And when Abram was ninety years old and nine, the LORD appeared to Abram, and said unto him, I am the Almighty God; walk before me, and be thou

perfect" (Genesis 17:1).

"I am the Alpha and Omega, the beginning and the ending, saith the Lord, which is, and which was, and which is to come, the Almighty." (Revelation 1:8).

"For the invisible things of him from the creation of the world are clearly seen, being understood by the things that are made, even his eternal power and Godhead; so that they are without excuse" (Romans 1:20).

"Is there anything too hard for the LORD?" (Genesis 18:14).

"And I will stretch out my hand and smite Egypt with all my wonders which I will do in the midst thereof: and after that he will let you go" (Exodus 3:20).

"Hast thou not known? Hast thou not heard, that the everlasting God, the LORD, the Creator of the ends of the earth, fainteth not, neither is weary" (Isaiah 40:28).

"Now unto him that is able to do exceedingly abundantly above all that we ask or think, according to the power that worketh in us" (Ephesians 3:20).

"Canst thou by searching find out God? Canst thou find out the Almighty unto perfection? It is as high as heaven; what canst thou do? Deeper than hell, what canst thou know? The measure thereof is longer than the earth, and broader than the sea. If he cut off, and shut up, or gather together, then who can hinder him? (Job 11:7).

Job realized that God is all-powerful:

"I know that thou canst do everything, and that no thought can be withholden from thee" (Job 42:2).

"By the word of the LORD were the heavens made; and all the host of them by the breath of his mouth" (Psalm 33:6).

God's power is beyond human comprehension:

"Touching the Almighty, we cannot find him out: he is excellent in power, and in judgement, and in plenty of justice: he will not afflict. Men do therefore fear him: he respecteth not any that are wise of heart" (Job 37:23-24).

"Trust ye in the LORD forever: for the LORD JEHOVAH is everlasting strength"(Isaiah 26:4).

"My counsel shall stand, and I will do all my pleasure" (Isaiah 46:10).

"For the LORD of hosts hath purposed, and who shall disannul it? And his hand is stretched out, and who shall turn it back?" (Isaiah 14:27).

"Mine hand also hath laid the foundation of the earth, and my right hand hath spanned the heavens: when I call unto them, they stand up together" (Isaiah 48:13).

Christians should have confidence in God's power:

"But our God is in the heavens; he hath done whatsoever he hath pleased" (Psalm 115:3).

"I can do all things through Christ which strengtheneth me" (Philippians 4:13).

"Who being the brightness of his glory, and the express image of his person, and upholding all things by the word of his power" (Hebrews 1:3).

"And he is before all things, and by him all things consist" (Colossians 1:17).

"Through faith we understand that the worlds were formed by the word of God, so that things which are seen were not made of things which do appear" (Hebrews 11:3).

Jesus taught:

> "With men this is impossible, but with God all things are possible" (Matthew 19:26).

> "Abba, Father, all things are possible unto thee, take away this cup from me; nevertheless not what I will, but what thou wilt" (Mark 14:36).

Gabriel, the angel, encouraged Mary with these words:

> "For with God nothing shall be impossible" (Luke 1:37).

God demonstrated His power over nature:

> "And he [Jesus] arose, and rebuked the wind, and said unto the sea, Peace be still. And the wind ceased, and there was a great calm. And he said unto them, Why are ye so fearful? How is it that ye have no faith? And they feared exceedingly, and said one to another, What manner of man is this, that even the wind and the sea obey him?" (Mark 4:39-41).

> "This the beginning of miracles did Jesus in Cana of Galilee and manifested forth his glory; and his disciples believed on him" (John 2:11).

Note this testimony of a man born blind but healed by Jesus:

> "Since the world began was it not heard that any man opened the eyes of one that was born blind. If this man were not of God, he could do nothing" (John 9:32-33).

While God is omnipotent, there are some things God *cannot* do:

God cannot lie:

> "In hope of eternal life, which God, that cannot lie, promised before the world began" (Titus 1:3).

> "That by two immutable things, in which it was impossible for God to lie, we might have a strong consolation, who have fled for refuge to lay hold upon the hope set before us" (Hebrews 6:18).

> "God is not a man, that he should lie; neither the son of man, that he should repent: hath he said, and shall he not do it? Or hath he spoken, and shall he not make it good?" (Numbers 23:19).

> "Also, the Strength of Israel will not lie" (1 Samuel 15:29).

God cannot increase or decrease in knowledge:

> "For if our heart condemn us, God is greater than our heart, and knoweth all things" (1 John 3:20).

God cannot be tempted with evil and cannot tempt others:

> "Let no man say when he is tempted, I am tempted of God. For God cannot be tempted with evil, neither tempteth he any man; but every man is tempted when is drawn away of his own lust and enticed" (James 1:13-14).

God cannot deny Himself:

"It is a faithful saying: For if we be dead with him, we shall also live with him. If we suffer, we shall also reign with him. If we deny him, he also will deny us. If we believe not, yet he abideth faithful: he cannot deny himself" (2 Timothy 2:11-13).

THE GOD OF THE KING JAMES BIBLE DOES NOT CHANGE

God is immutable. He is the absolute. He is the ideal. He is the perfect One.

> "And this is eternal life, that they may know thee the only true God, and Jesus Christ whom thou hast sent. . . . And now, O Father, glorify thou me with thine own self with the glory which I had with thee before the world was" (John 17:3-5).

> "I said, O my God, take me not away in the midst of my days: thy years are throughout all generations. Of old hast thou laid the foundation of the earth: and the heavens are the work of thy hands. They shall perish, but thou shall endure: yea, all of them shall wax old like a garment; as a vesture shalt thou change them, and they shall be changed. But thou art the same, and thy years shall have no end" (Psalm 102:24-27).

> "The counsel of the LORD standeth forever, the thoughts of his heart to all generations" (Psalm 33:11).

> "For I am the LORD, I change not; therefore ye sons of Jacob are not consumed" (Malachi 3:6).

> ". . . even his eternal power and Godhead." (Romans 1:20).

"Every good gift and every perfect gift is from above, and cometh down from the Father of lights, with whom is no variableness, neither shadow of turning" (James 1:17).

"But unto the Son he saith: Thy throne, O God, is for ever and ever . . . as a vesture shalt thou fold them up, and they shall be changed, but Thou are the same, and Thy years shall not fail . . . sit on my right hand, until I make Thine enemies Thy footstool" (Hebrews 1:8-13).

"Jesus Christ the same yesterday, and today, and forever" (Hebrews 13:8).

In the last chapter of the King James Bible, Jesus declared, "I am Alpha and Omega, the beginning and the end, the first and the last" (Revelation 22:13).

THE GOD OF THE KING JAMES BIBLE IS THE GOD OF TRUTH

God is truth. He is the source of truth and the standard by which people must judge what is true and what is false. And He is the One who enables people to know the truth.

> "Thou shalt not bear false witness against thy neighbor" (Exodus 20:16).

> "And the Word was made flesh, and dwelt among us, (and we beheld his glory, the glory as of the only begotten of the Father) full of grace and truth" (John 1:14).

> "For the law was given by Moses, but grace and truth came by Jesus Christ" (John 1:17).

> "He that hath received his testimony hath set to his seal that God is true" (John 3:33).

> "God is a Spirit: and they that worship him must worship him in spirit and truth" (John 4:24).

> "Then said Jesus to those Jews which believed on him, If ye continue in my word, then are ye my disciples indeed. And ye shall know the truth, and the truth shall make you free" (John 8:31-32).

"Jesus saith unto him, I am the way, the truth, and the life: no man cometh unto the Father, but by me" (John 14:6).

"Howbeit when he, the Spirit of truth, is come, he will guide you into all truth: for he shall not speak of himself; but whatsoever he shall hear, that shall he speak: and he will shew you things to come" (John 16:13).

"Sanctify them through thy truth: thy word is truth (John 17:17).

"Seeing ye have purified your souls in obeying the truth through the Spirit unto unfeigned love of the brethren, see that ye love one another with a pure heart fervently" (1 Peter 1:22).

"To this end was I born, and for this cause came I into the world, that I should bear witness unto the truth. Every one that is of the truth heareth my voice (John 18:37).

"But we are sure that the judgement of God is according to truth against them which commit such things" (Romans 2:2).

"God forbid: yea, let God be true, and every man a liar" (Romans 3:4).

"And Jesus answered and said unto him, Blessed art thou, Simon Barjona: for flesh and blood hath not revealed it unto thee, but my Father which is in heaven" (Matthew 16:17).

"But God hath revealed them unto us by his Spirit" (1 Corinthians 2:10).

"Charity . . . rejoiceth not in iniquity, but rejoiceth in the truth" (1 Corinthians 13:4-6).

"In whom ye also trusted, after that ye heard the word of truth, the gospel of your salvation: in whom also after that ye believed, ye were sealed with that holy Spirit of promise" (Ephesians 1:13).

"And the LORD passed by before him, and proclaimed, The LORD, The LORD God, merciful and gracious, longsuffering, and abundant in goodness and truth" (Exodus 34:6).

"That he who blesseth himself in the earth shall bless himself in the God of truth" (Isaiah 65:16).

"Now for a long season Israel hath been without the true God, and without a teaching priest, and without law" (2 Chronicles 15:3).

"Into thine hand I commit my spirit: thou hast redeemed me, O LORD God of truth" (Psalm 31:5).

"For the wrath of God is revealed from heaven against all ungodliness and unrighteousness of me, who hold (suppress) the truth in unrighteousness" (Roman 1:18).

God's truthfulness and His being the absolute standard for truth is emphasized in James 1 and elsewhere:

> "Every good gift and every perfect gift is from above, and cometh down from the Father of lights, with whom is no variableness, neither shadow of turning. Of his own free will begat he us with the word of truth" (James 1:17-18).

> "For thy mercy is great unto the heavens, and thy truth unto the clouds" (Psalm 57:10).

> "All the paths of the LORD are mercy and truth unto such as keep his covenant and his testimonies" (Psalm 25:10).

> "Thus saith the LORD; I am returned unto Zion, and will dwell in the midst of Jerusalem: and Jerusalem shall be called a city of truth; and the mountain of the LORD of hosts the holy mountain" (Zachariah 7:10).

> "And we know that the Son of God is come, and hath given us an understanding, that we may know him that is true, and we are in him that is true, even in his Son Jesus Christ. This is the true God, and eternal life (1 John 5:20).

> "In hope of eternal life, which God, that cannot lie, promised before the world began" (Titus 1:2).

"That by two immutable things, in which it was impossible for God to lie, we might have a strong consolation, who have fled for refuge to lay hold upon the hope set before us (Hebrews 6:18).

THE GOD OF THE KING JAMES BIBLE IS LOVE

"Beloved, let us love one another: for love is of God; and everyone that loveth is born of God, and knoweth God. He that loveth not knoweth not God; for God is love" (1 John 4:7-8).

"For God so loved the world, that he gave his only begotten Son, that whosoever believeth in him should not perish, but have everlasting life" (John 3:16).

"And Jesus answered him, The first of all commandments is, HEAR, O ISRAEL; THE LORD OUR GOD IS ONE LORD: AND THOU SHALT LOVE THE LORD THY GOD WITH ALL THY HEART, AND WITH ALL THY SOUL, AND WITH ALL THY MIND, AND WITH ALL THY STRENTH: this is the first commandment. And the second is like, namely this: THOU SHALT LOVE THY NEIGHBOR AS THYSELF. There is none other commandment greater than these" (Mark 12:29-31).

The law came from God and love is the fulfillment of the law:

"Love worketh no ill to his neighbor: therefore love is the fulfilling of the law" (Romans 13:10).

"Know therefore that the LORD thy God, he is God, the faithful God, which keepeth covenant and mercy with them that love him and keep his commandments to a thousand generations" (Deuteronomy 7:9).

Jesus said, "Come unto me all ye that labor and are heavy laden, and I will give you rest. Take my yoke upon you and learn of me; for I am meek and lowly in heart: and ye shall find rest unto your souls. For my yoke is easy, and my burden is light" (Matthew 11:28-30).

"But God commendeth his love toward us, in that, while we were yet sinners Christ died for us" (Romans 5:8).

"And hope maketh not ashamed; because the love of God is shed abroad in our hearts by the Holy Ghost which is given unto us" (Romans 5:5).

"But thou, O LORD, art a God full of compassion, and gracious, longsuffering, and plenteous in mercy and truth" (Psalm 86:15).

"For the LORD is good; his mercy is everlasting; and his truth endureth to all generations (Psalm 100:5).

"O give thanks unto the God of heaven: for his mercy endureth forever" (Psalm 136:26).

"The LORD thy God in the midst of thee is mighty; he will save, he will rejoice over thee with joy; he will rest in his love, he will joy over thee with singing" (Zephaniah 3:17).

"And lo a voice from heaven, saying, This is my beloved Son, in whom I am well pleased" (Matthew 3:17).

"I am the good shepherd: the good shepherd giveth his life for the sheep" (John 10:11).

"Greater love hath no man than this: that a man lay down his life for his friends" (John 15:13).

"Hereby perceive we the love of God, because he laid down his life for us: and we ought to lay down our lives for the brethren" (1 John 3:16).

"Who shall separate us from the love of Christ? Shall tribulation, or distress, or persecution, or famine, or nakedness, or peril, or sword? . . . Nay, in all these things we are more than conquerors through him that loved us. For I am persuaded that neither death, nor life, nor angels, nor principalities, nor powers, nor things present, nor things to come, nor height, nor depth, nor any other creature, shall be able to separate us from the love of God which is in Christ Jesus our Lord" (Romans 8:35-39.)

Isaiah compares God's love to the love of a mother for her nursing child: Isaiah 49:15:

"Can a woman forget her sucking child, that she should not have compassion on the son of her womb? yea, they may forget, yet will I not forget thee."

God's love is in His presence:

"In all their affliction he was afflicted, and the angel of his presence saved them: in his love and in his pity he redeemed them; and he bore them, and carried them all the days of old" (Isaiah 63:9).

"The LORD hath appeared of old unto me, saying, Yes I have loved thee with an everlasting love: therefore with lovingkindness have I drawn thee" (Jeremiah 31:3).

"And now abideth faith, hope, charity, these three; but the greatest of these is charity" (1 Corinthians 13:3).

"And above all things have fervent charity among yourselves: for CHARITY SHALL COVER THE MULTITUDE OF SINS" (1 Peter 4:8).

"Husbands, love your wives, even as Christ also loved the church and gave himself for it" (Ephesians 5:25).

"Casting all your care upon him [God], for he careth for you" (1 Peter 5:7).

THE GOD OF THE KING JAMES BIBLE IS GRACIOUS, MERCIFUL, AND KIND

"Grace be to you and peace from God our Father and from the Lord Jesus Christ. Blessed be the God and Father of our Lord Jesus Christ, who hath blessed us with all spiritual blessings in heavenly places in Christ" (Ephesians 1:2-3).

"But God who is rich in mercy, for his great love wherewith he loved us . . . that in the ages to come he might shew the exceeding riches of his grace in his kindness toward us through Christ Jesus. For by grace ye saved through faith; and that not of yourselves: it is the gift of God: not of works, lest any man should boast" (Ephesians 2:4-9).

"Grace be with all them that love our Lord Jesus Christ in sincerity. Amen" (Ephesians 6:24).

"And the LORD passed by before him (Moses) and proclaimed, The LORD, The LORD GOD, merciful and gracious, longsuffering, and abundant in goodness and truth—keeping mercy for thousands, forgiving iniquity and transgression and sin, and that will by no means clear the guilty" (Exodus 34:6-7).

"Or despises thou the riches of his goodness (kindness) and forbearance and longsuffering; not knowing that the goodness of God leadeth thee to repentance?" (Romans 2:4).

"But Noah found grace in the eyes of the LORD" (Genesis 6:8).

"And the angel said unto her, Fear not, Mary: for thou hast found favor with God" (Luke 1:30).

"To give knowledge of salvation unto his people by the remission of their sins through the tender mercy of our God" (Luke 1:77-78).

"Be ye merciful, as your Father also is merciful" (Luke 6:36).

"And the Word was made flesh, and dwelt among us, (and we beheld his glory, the glory as of the only begotten of the Father,) full of grace and truth" (John 1:14).

"And of his fulness have all we received, and grace for grace. For the law was given by Moses, but grace and truth came by Jesus Christ" (John 1:16-17).

"Being justified freely by his grace through the redemption that is in Christ Jesus" (Romans 3:24).

"To Timothy, my dearly beloved son: Grace, mercy, and peace from God the Father and Christ Jesus our Lord" (2 Timothy 1:2).

"Let us therefore come boldly unto the throne of grace, that we may obtain mercy and find grace to help in time of need" (Hebrews 4:16).

"But we see Jesus, who was made a little lower than the angels for the suffering of death, crowned with glory and honor; that he by the grace of God should taste death for every man" (Hebrews 2:9).

"But thou art a God ready to pardon, gracious and merciful, slow to anger, and of great kindness" (Nehemiah 9:17).

"Because thy lovingkindness is better than life, my lips shall praise thee" (Psalm 63:3).

"He hath remembered his mercy and his truth toward the house of Israel: all the ends of the earth have seen the salvation of our God" (Psalm 98:3).

"The LORD hath appeared of old unto me saying, Yea, I have loved thee with an everlasting love: therefore with lovingkindness have I drawn thee" (Jeremiah 31:3).

"Blessed be the God and Father of our Lord Jesus Christ which according to his abundant mercy hath begotten us again unto a lively hope by the resurrection of Jesus Christ from the dead" (1 Peter 1:3).

"John to the seven churches which are in Asia: Grace be unto you and peace from him which is, and which was, and which is to come; and from the seven Spirits which are before his throne" (Revelation 1:4).

"Grace be to you and peace from God the Father and from the Lord Jesus Christ" (Ephesians 1:2).

"For the grace of God that bringeth salvation hath appeared to all men" (Titus 2:11).

"He that oppresseth the poor reproacheth his Maker: but he that honoureth him hath mercy on the poor" (Proverbs 14:31).

"The LORD is gracious and full of compassion; slow to anger and of great mercy. The LORD is good to all: and his tender mercies are over all his works" (Psalm 145:8-9).

"Mercy rejoiceth against judgement" (James 2:13b).

"The LORD make his face shine upon thee and be gracious unto thee" (Numbers 6:25).

"And Jesus, when he came out, saw much people and was moved with compassion toward them, because they were as sheep not having a shepherd" (Mark 6:34).

"And the word of the LORD came unto Zachariah, saying, Thus speaketh the LORD of hosts, saying, Execute true judgement and shew mercy and compassion every man to his brother: and oppress not the widow, nor the fatherless, the stranger, nor the poor; and let none of you imagine evil against his brother in your heart" (Zechariah 7:8-10).

THE GOD OF THE KING JAMES BIBLE IS JESUS CHRIST

Jesus is called God:

> "In the beginning was the Word (Jesus), and the Word was with God, and the Word was God" (John 1:1).

Jesus is the unique Son of God, and Sonship denotes equality with God the Father, not inferiority:

> "But Jesus answered them, My father worketh hitherto, and I work. Therefore the Jews sought the more to kill him, because he not only had broken the sabbath, but said God was his Father, making himself equal with God" (John 5:17-18).

> "Jesus said unto them, Verily, verily, I say unto you, Before Abraham was, I am" (John 8:58).

Jesus said, "I and my Father are one" (John 10:30).

> "The Jews answered him, saying, For a good work we stone thee not: but for blasphemy; and because that thou, being a man, makest thyself God" (John 10:33).

> "And Thomas answered and said unto him, My LORD and my God" (John 20:28).

The name "Jesus" means "Jehovah is salvation" or "Jehovah saves."

"And she shall bring forth a son, and thou shalt call his name JESUS: for he shall save his people from their sins" (Matthew 1:21).

"Behold, a virgin shall be with child and shall bring forth a son, and they shall call his name Emmanuel, which being interpreted is, God with us" (Matthew 1:23).

"And, behold, thou shalt conceive in thy womb, and bring forth a son, and shalt call his name JESUS" (Luke 1:31).

"He shall be great and shall be called the Son of the Highest: and the Lord God shall give unto him the throne of his father David" (Luke 1:32).

"And the angel answered and said unto her, The Holy Ghost shall come upon thee, and the power of the Highest shall overshadow thee: therefore also that holy thing which shall be born of thee shall be called the Son of God" (Luke 1:35).

"Then they (the disciples) that were in the ship came and worshipped him (Jesus), saying, Of a truth thou art the Son of God" (Matthew 14:33).

"And Jesus said unto him, Why callest thou me good? There is none good but one, that is, God" (Mark 10:18).

"When Jesus saw their faith, he said unto the sick of the palsy, Son, thy sins be forgiven thee. But there were certain of the scribes sitting there, and reasoning in their hearts, Why doth this man thus speak blasphemies? Who can forgive sins but God only?" (Mark 2:5-7)

"Take heed therefore unto yourselves, and to all the flock, over the which the Holy Ghost hath made you overseers, to feed the church of God, which he hath purchased with his own blood" (Acts 20:28).

"Who are Israelites; to whom pertaineth the adoption, and the glory, and the covenants, and the giving of the law, and the service of God, and the promises. Whose are the fathers, and of whom as concerning the flesh Christ came, who is over all, God blessed forever. Amen" (Romans 9:4-5).

"Looking for that blessed hope, and the glorious appearing of the great God and our Savior Jesus Christ" (Titus 2:13).

"Let this mind be in you, which was also in Christ Jesus: Who, being in the form of God, thought it not robbery to be equal with God: But made himself of no reputation, and took upon him the form of a servant, and was made in the likeness of men: And being found in fashion as a man, he humbled himself, and became obedient unto death, even the death of the cross. Wherefore, God also hath highly exalted him, and given him a name which is above every name: That at the name of Jesus every knee should bow, of things in heaven, and things in earth, and things under the earth. And that every tongue should confess that Jesus Christ is Lord, to the glory of God the Father" (Philippians 2:5-11).

"Who is the image of the invisible God, the firstborn of every creature" (Colossians 1:15).

"For in him dwelleth all the fullness of the Godhead bodily" (Colossians 2:9).

"But unto the Son he saith, THY THRONE, O GOD, IS FOR EVER AND EVER: A SCEPTRE OF RIGHTEOUSNESS IS THE SCEPTRE OF THY KINGDOM (Hebrews 1:8).

"Simon Peter, a servant and an apostle of Jesus Christ, to them that have obtained like precious faith with us through the righteousness of God and our Savior Jesus Christ" (2 Peter 1:1).

"For many deceivers are entered into the world, who confess not that Jesus Christ is come in the flesh. This is a deceiver and an antichrist" (2 John 7).

"Whosoever transgresseth, and abideth not in the doctrine of Christ, hath not God. He that abideth in the doctrine of Christ, he hath both the Father and the Son" (2 John 9).

"[Jesus said,] I am Alpha and Omega, the beginning and the end, the first and the last" (Revelation 22:13).

"And we know that the Son of God is come, and hath given us an understanding, that we may know him that is true, and we are in him that is true, even in his Son Jesus Christ. This is the true God, and eternal life" (1 John 5:20).

THE GOD OF THE KING JAMES BIBLE IS LIKE A SHEPHERD:

"I am the good shepherd: the good shepherd giveth his life for the sheep. But he that is an hireling, and not the shepherd, whose own the sheep are not, seeth the wolf coming, and leaveth the sheep, and fleeth: and the wolf catchet them, and scattereth the sheep. The hireling fleeth, because he is an hireling, and careth not for the sheep. I am the good shepherd, and know my sheep, and am known of mine.

"As the Father knoweth me, even so know I the Father: and I lay down my life for the sheep. And other sheep I have, which are not of this fold: them also I must bring, and they shall hear my voice; and there shall be one fold, and one shepherd. Therefore doth my Father love me, because I lay down my life, that I might take it again.

"No man taketh it from me, but I lay it down of myself. I have power to lay it down, and I have power to take it again. This commandment have I received of my Father" (John 10: 11-18).

God shepherds the lives of all who call on the name of the Lord Jesus Christ:

"The Lord is my shepherd; I shall not want. He maketh me to lie down in green pastures: he leadeth me beside the still waters. He restoreth my soul: he leadeth me in the paths of righteousness for his name's sake.

"Yea, though I walk through the valley of the shadow of death, I will fear no evil: for thou art with me; thy rod and thy staff they shall comfort me.

"Thou preparest a table before me in the presence of mine enemies: thou anointest my head with oil; my cup runneth over. Surely goodness and mercy shall follow me all the days of my life: and I will dwell in the house of the Lord forever" (Psalm 23).

REFERENCES

Lawson, Steve. *The Attributes of God*. Sanford, Florida: Ligonier, 2013.

McClain, Alva J. "God and Revelation," Classroom syllabus. Winona Lake, Indiana: Grace Theological Seminary, n.d.

The Thompson Chain-Reference Bible. Indianapolis: B.B. Kirkbride, 2007.

ABOUT THE AUTHOR

James Coffey has a very broad educational background. He graduated from Mercer University with a bachelor of arts in history and art. At Mercer he played on the varsity golf team. James earned his English Education Certificate from Grace College and graduated from Grace Theological Seminary with a Certificate in Biblical Studies. He taught English as a Second Language in Knoxville, Tennessee and regularly wrote "The Jewish Aspect" for The Bible Expositor and Illuminator. He currently lives in Georgia with his wife.

Printed in the United States
By Bookmasters